TRANSFORMERS ANIMATED ™

HOW TO DRAW

By Sadie Chesterfield
Illustrated by Carlo LoRaso

HarperCollins *Children's Books*

Tools of the Trade

Soon you will be transported into the future, where a band of Autobots must battle villains to protect the earth. But before you learn to draw your favourite *Transformers Animated* characters, you'll need some basic art supplies. Grab a pencil, a rubber, and a pencil sharpener. To add colour to your drawings, find some felt-tip pens, coloured pencils, or paint. You may also want to use graph paper to help guide you through each step.

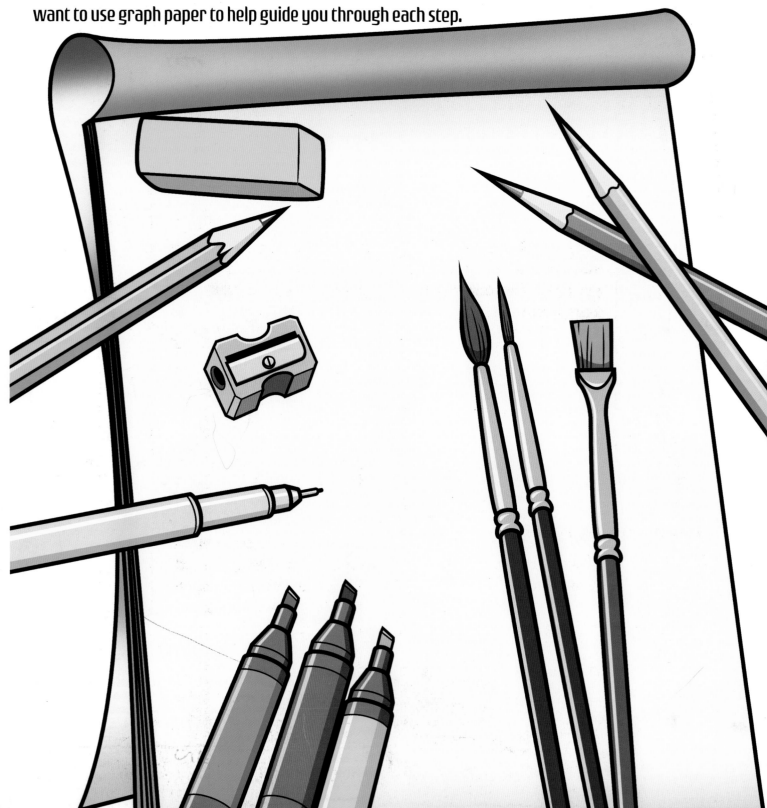

Step-by-Step

You can draw any *Transformers Animated* character by following these simple steps.

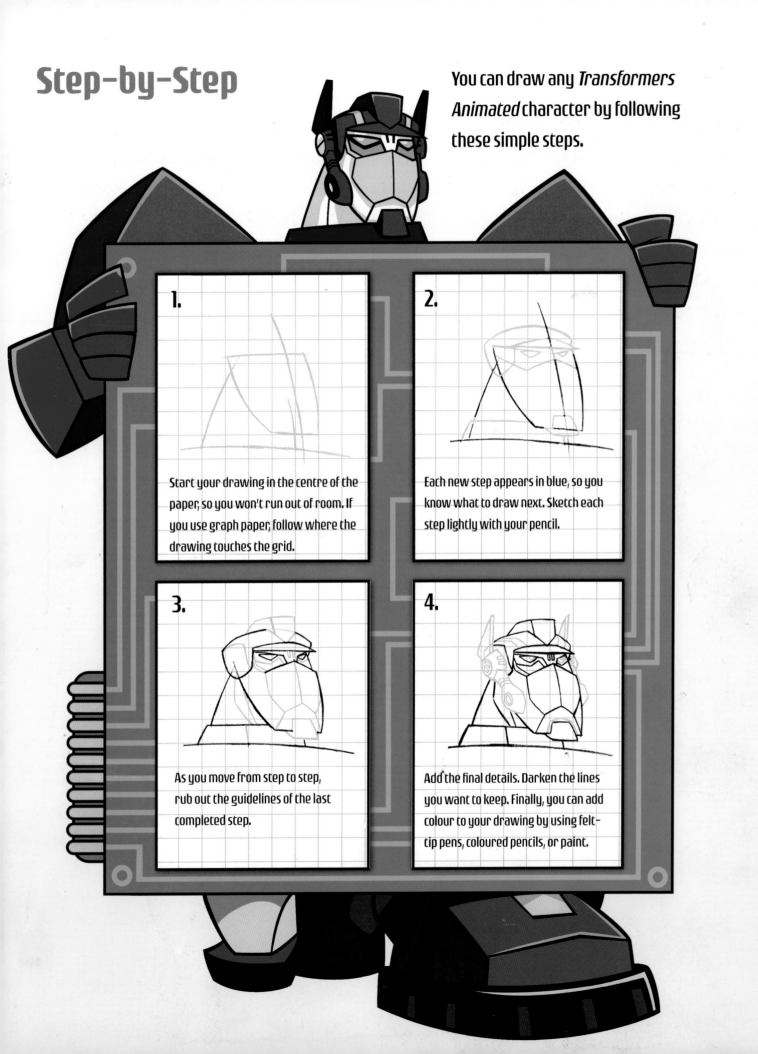

1.
Start your drawing in the centre of the paper, so you won't run out of room. If you use graph paper, follow where the drawing touches the grid.

2.
Each new step appears in blue, so you know what to draw next. Sketch each step lightly with your pencil.

3.
As you move from step to step, rub out the guidelines of the last completed step.

4.
Add the final details. Darken the lines you want to keep. Finally, you can add colour to your drawing by using felt-tip pens, coloured pencils, or paint.

The Cast

The best artists pay close attention to proportions (or the size of a character compared to the objects around it). You'll notice Prowl and Ratchet are almost the same height, while Megatron is about twice their size. When you draw these characters next to each other, check this chart to make sure your proportions are correct.

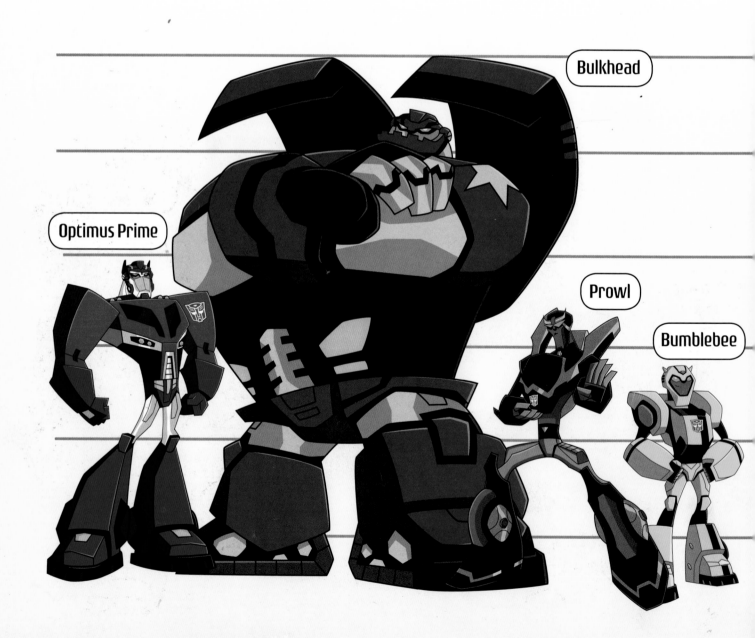

Bulkhead

Optimus Prime

Prowl

Bumblebee

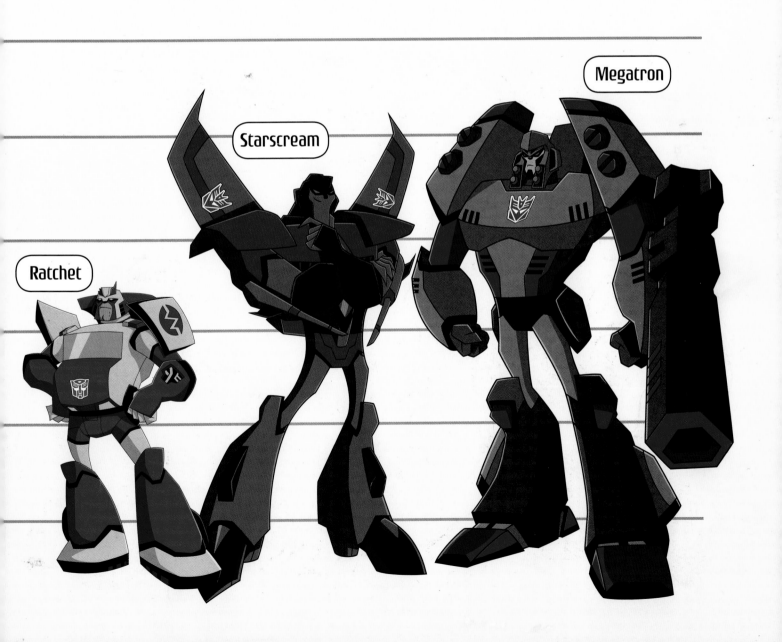

Ratchet

Starscream

Megatron

Optimus Prime

Optimus Prime is a walking utility belt, equipped with every tool you can imagine. Smoke screen? Hang glider? Fire extinguisher? Axe? Prime has them all.

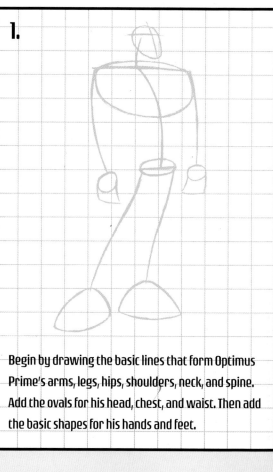

1.

Begin by drawing the basic lines that form Optimus Prime's arms, legs, hips, shoulders, neck, and spine. Add the ovals for his head, chest, and waist. Then add the basic shapes for his hands and feet.

2.

Fill out Prime's arms and legs by drawing ovals. These ovals should meet at his joints. Add two more ovals to fill out his neck and stomach.

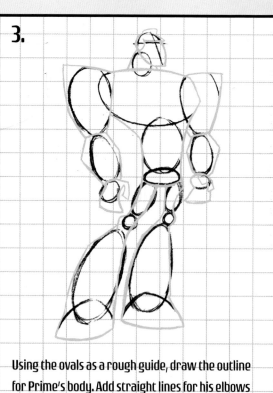

3.

Using the ovals as a rough guide, draw the outline for Prime's body. Add straight lines for his elbows and wrists. Don't forget to draw his helmet and thumbs!

4.

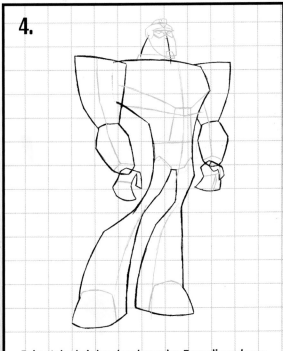

Prime's body is hard and angular. Draw lines down his arms and legs and across his chest. Separate his legs from his feet, and add the details on his face and hands.

5.

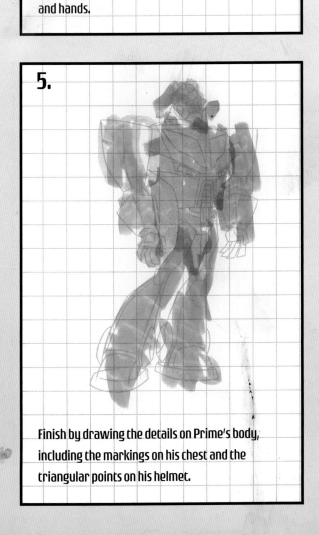

Finish by drawing the details on Prime's body, including the markings on his chest and the triangular points on his helmet.

Follow these steps to draw Prime's axe:

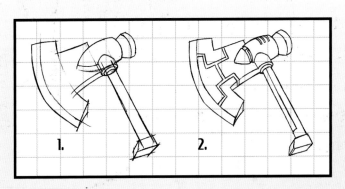

1.

2.

6. Then, just add some colour!

Optimus Prime Vehicle Mode: The Fire Truck

Since they have become heroes on Earth, the Autobots get recognized everywhere! The fire truck isn't just a faster way for Optimus Prime to get around; it's also his secret identity. He can sneak up on enemies for a surprise attack, or simply drive around Detroit, hidden in plain sight.

1.

Begin by drawing the outline of the truck. It's pointed in the front, like a triangle. Add the guidelines for the windshield and door.

2.

Draw two lines on the side of the truck, and outline the windshield and the grill.

3.

Add the details on the front. Add the bumper and the two large wheels.

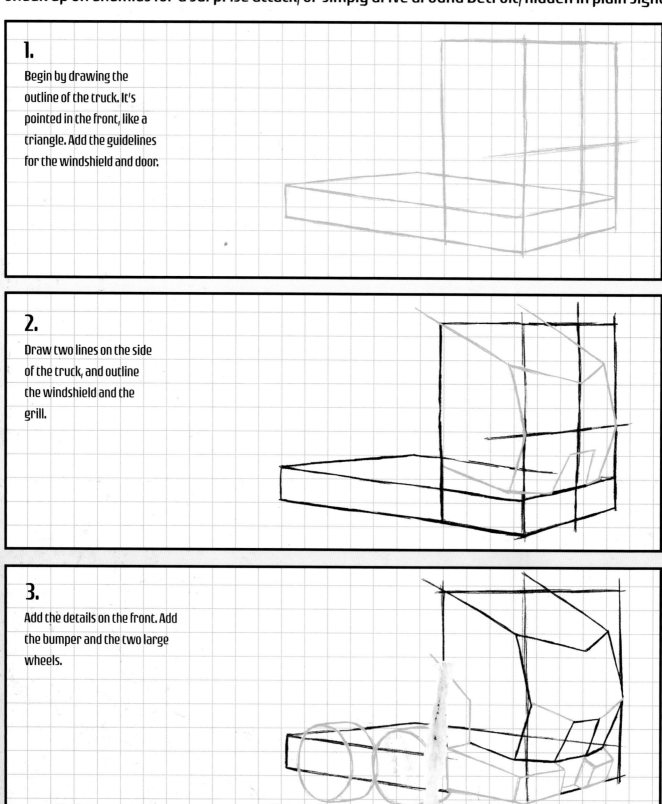

4.

Add two circles for each wheel, and the details on the grill and windshield.

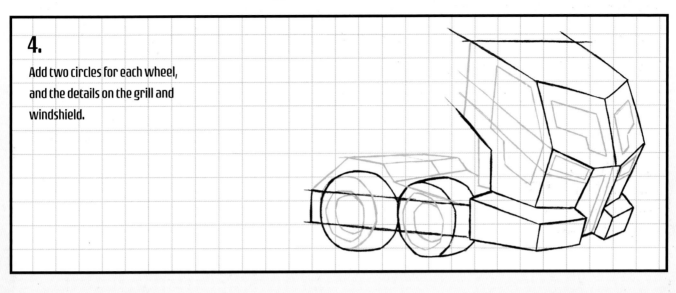

5.

Finish your drawing by adding the last details.

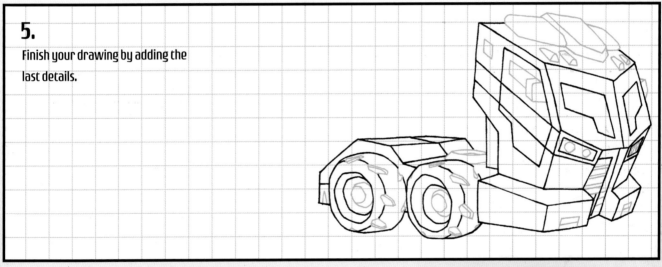

6.

Now you can colour the fire truck a bright red!

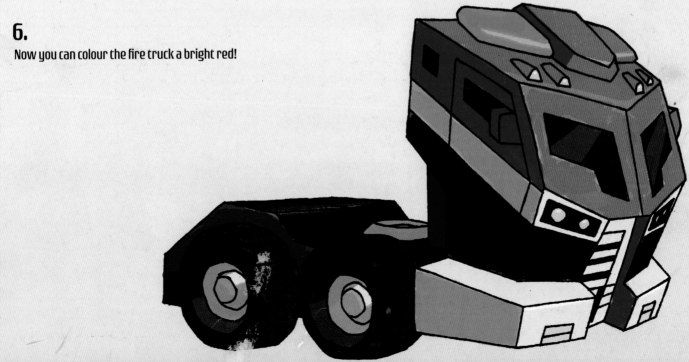

Megatron

Megatron is the leader of the Decepticons, a group of Transformers bent on destruction. While the Autobots protect humans, Megatron has no concern for human life. A savage fighter, he is determined to destroy any Autobot he encounters.

1.

Begin by drawing the basic lines that form Megatron's arms, legs, hips, shoulders, and spine. Add ovals for his head, chest, and waist. Then add the ovals for his hands and flattened ovals for his feet.

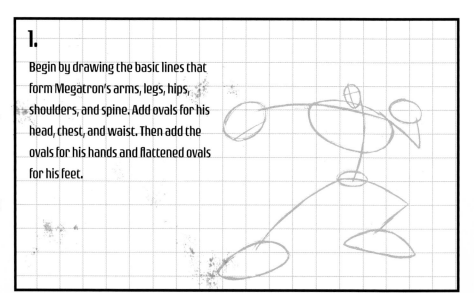

2.

Fill out Megatron's arms and legs by adding ovals. They should meet at the joints. Add a circle around his head and another for his shoulder. Connect the ovals that form Megatron's chest and waist with two curved lines.

3.

Using the ovals as a guide, draw the outline of Megatron's body. In this pose, Megatron's legs form a slight arch. Don't forget to add the details for his helmet!

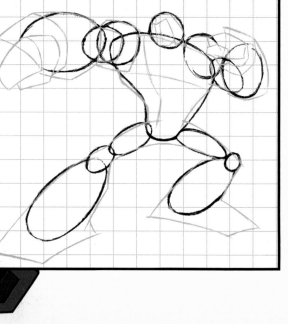

4.

Megatron's body is hard and angular. Add a line connecting his fist to his elbow, and two more connecting each toe to his bent knee. Draw a line down the centre of his chest and add the details on his fists.

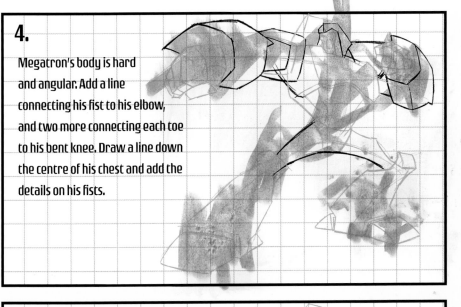

5.

Divide Megatron's fists into curled fingers. Separate his legs from his feet and his chest from his stomach. Don't forget to add the details of his face!

6.

Finally, add the details on his body, and then just add colour!

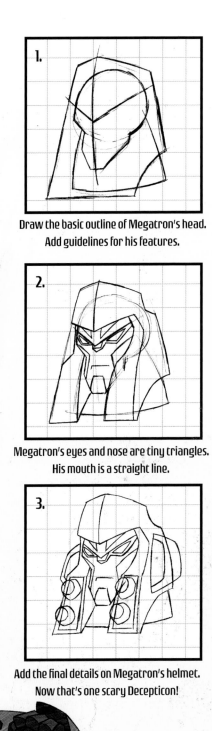

1.

Draw the basic outline of Megatron's head. Add guidelines for his features.

2.

Megatron's eyes and nose are tiny triangles. His mouth is a straight line.

3.

Add the final details on Megatron's helmet. Now that's one scary Decepticon!

The Helicopter

Decepticons have secret identities, too. Megatron's vehicle mode is a helicopter gunship. Follow the steps below to draw a Decepticon in hiding.

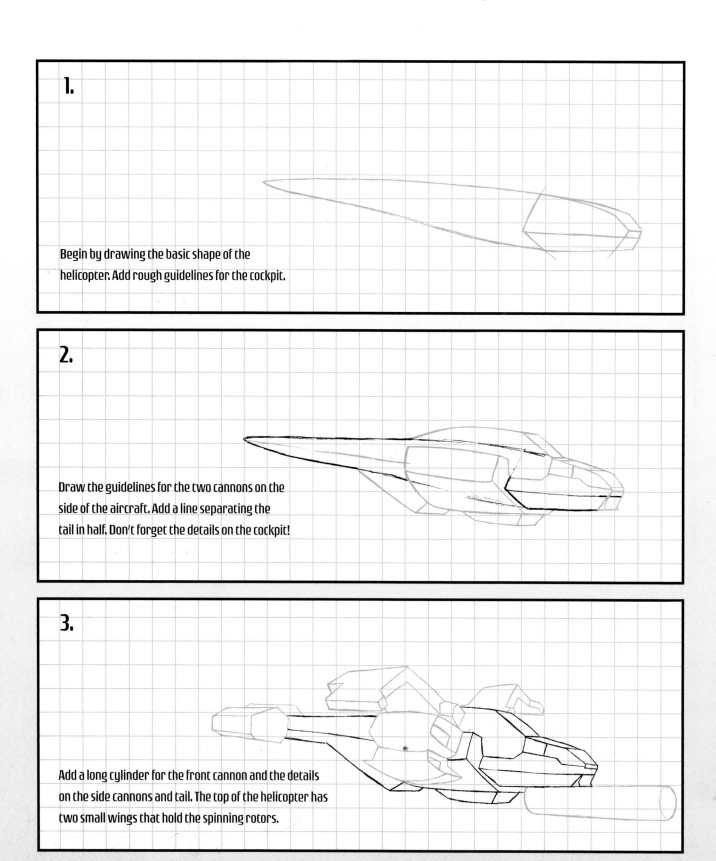

1.

Begin by drawing the basic shape of the helicopter. Add rough guidelines for the cockpit.

2.

Draw the guidelines for the two cannons on the side of the aircraft. Add a line separating the tail in half. Don't forget the details on the cockpit!

3.

Add a long cylinder for the front cannon and the details on the side cannons and tail. The top of the helicopter has two small wings that hold the spinning rotors.

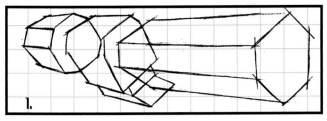

To draw Megatron's cannon, start with these basic, overlapping shapes.

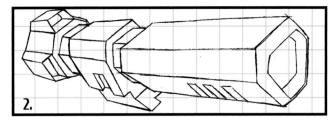

Finish the drawing by adding these details. Megatron takes aim!

4.

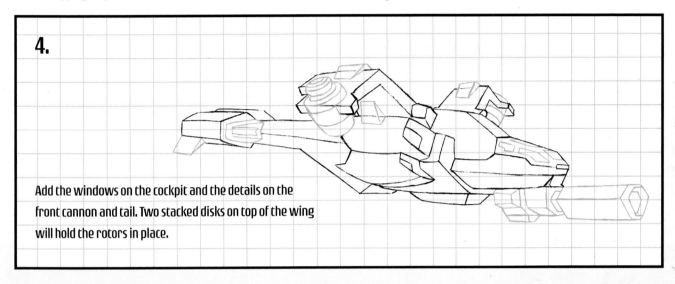

Add the windows on the cockpit and the details on the front cannon and tail. Two stacked disks on top of the wing will hold the rotors in place.

5.

Draw the two long slats that create the rotors. Add the final details.

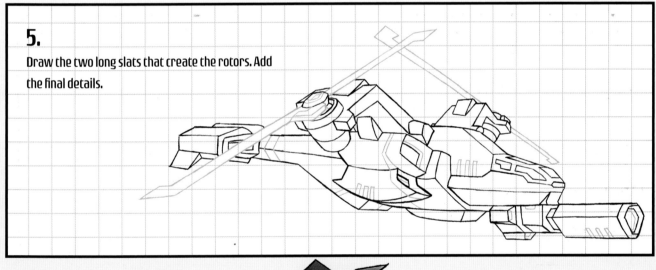

6.

Finally, add colour. Watch out, Autobots... this helicopter is ready for takeoff!

Prowl

Prowl is an expert at camouflaging himself and can turn almost any ordinary object into a weapon. He would rather meditate in his bonsai garden or save a stray animal than bask in human attention. He doesn't like being called a superhero; he's just doing what's right.

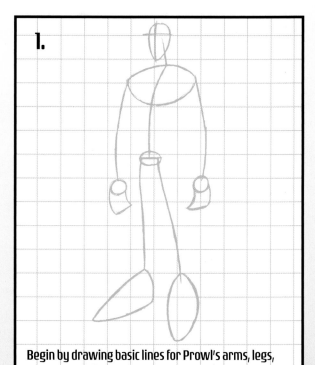

1. Begin by drawing basic lines for Prowl's arms, legs, shoulders, neck, hips, and spine. Add ovals for his head, chest, and waist. Lastly, sketch the basic shapes for his hands and feet.

2. Start filling out Prowl's arms and legs with ovals. Add two circles for his shoulders, and one for his neck. Prowl is narrow! Extend his chest with a curved line and add a tiny oval for his stomach.

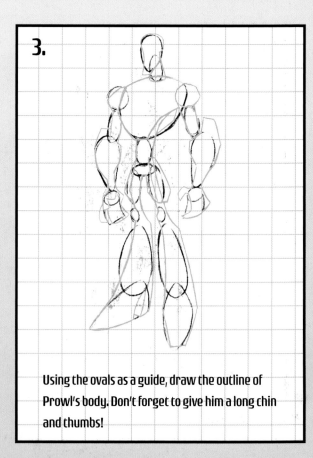

3. Using the ovals as a guide, draw the outline of Prowl's body. Don't forget to give him a long chin and thumbs!

4.

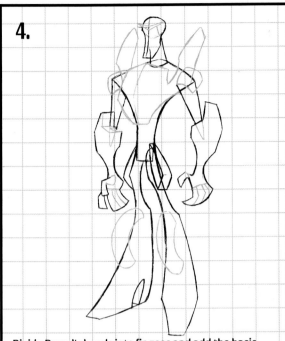

Divide Prowl's hands into fingers and add the basic shapes for the wheels on his legs. Add the caps on his shoulders and the blades that extend upward from them. Lastly, add his eyes.

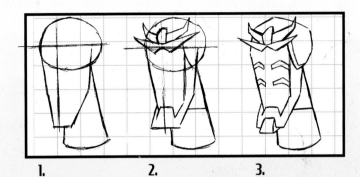

1.
Now try drawing Prowl's mask in ninja mode. Start with the basic shapes of his head. Add the guidelines for his features.

2.
Prowl's eyes are two overlapping triangles. His chin is separate from his face, like a beard.

3.
Add a square on Prowl's chin and define his helmet. When his mask is up, there are four short lines on his face.

5.

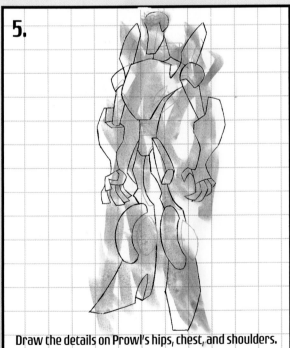

Draw the details on Prowl's hips, chest, and shoulders. On each leg, draw a football shape. This will become the center of his wheels. Be sure to add the details around Prowl's eyes!

6.

Finish your drawing by adding the final details on Prowl's suit. Now it's time to give this Autobot some colour!

The Motorcycle

In vehicle form, Prowl is a fast, sleek motorcycle. A natural spy, he uses his secret identity to sneak into any location unseen and unheard.

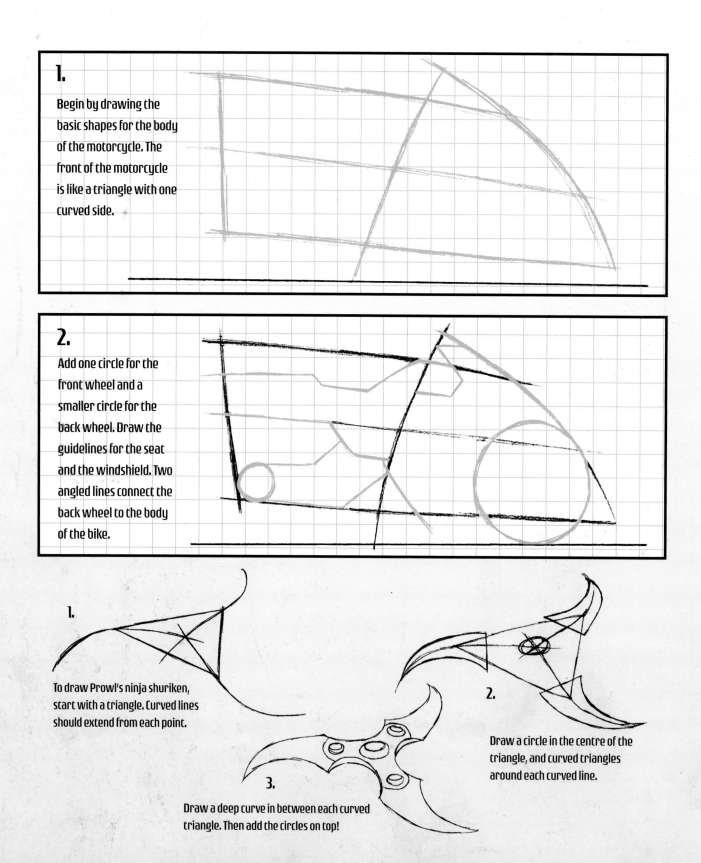

1.

Begin by drawing the basic shapes for the body of the motorcycle. The front of the motorcycle is like a triangle with one curved side.

2.

Add one circle for the front wheel and a smaller circle for the back wheel. Draw the guidelines for the seat and the windshield. Two angled lines connect the back wheel to the body of the bike.

1.

To draw Prowl's ninja shuriken, start with a triangle. Curved lines should extend from each point.

2.

Draw a circle in the centre of the triangle, and curved triangles around each curved line.

3.

Draw a deep curve in between each curved triangle. Then add the circles on top!

3.

Using the guidelines you made in the second step, divide the seat into six sections. Add the back of the seat and a small circle for the handlebar. Draw the outside circle of the back tyre and connect the front tyre to the bike.

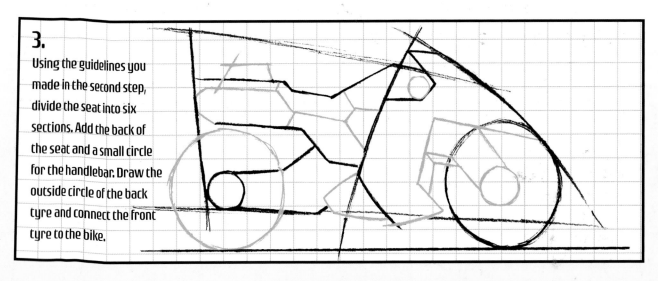

4.

Finish by adding the details on the tyres, seat, and windshield. Add two circles inside the handlebar to create depth.

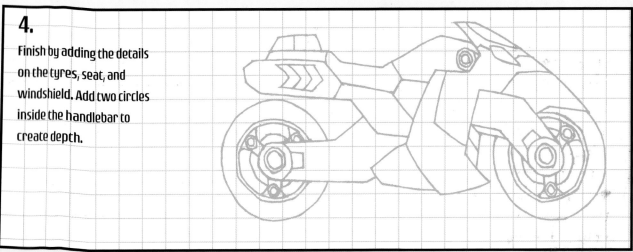

5.

Now add **some** colour to make this motorcycle shine!

Starscream

Starscream's wings allow him to fly rings around the Autobots. In battle, Starscream produces a sonic scream so powerful its sound can send enemies spinning through the air.

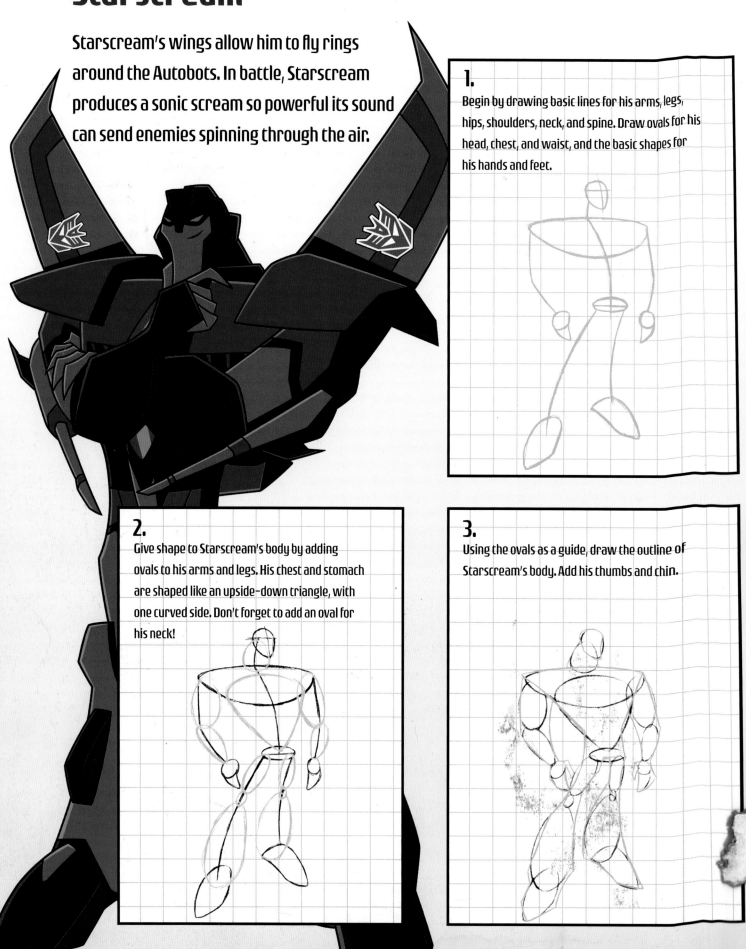

1.
Begin by drawing basic lines for his arms, legs, hips, shoulders, neck, and spine. Draw ovals for his head, chest, and waist, and the basic shapes for his hands and feet.

2.
Give shape to Starscream's body by adding ovals to his arms and legs. His chest and stomach are shaped like an upside-down triangle, with one curved side. Don't forget to add an oval for his neck!

3.
Using the ovals as a guide, draw the outline of Starscream's body. Add his thumbs and chin.

4.

Add triangles across his shoulders and the details of his face. Starscream's forearms stick out from his arm, just like his knees stick out from his legs. Draw two intersecting lines across his chest.

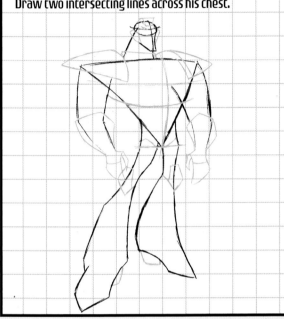

5.

Draw wings and divide hands into fingers. Add the details on his chest and legs, and blasters on each arm.

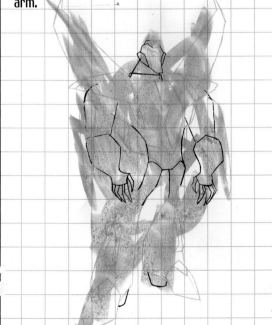

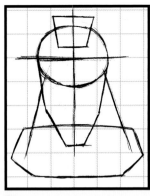

1.
To draw Starscream's face, sketch the basic shapes of his head and the guidelines for his features.

2.
Starscream is always scheming. Draw his mischievous expression. His mouth slants toward the left.

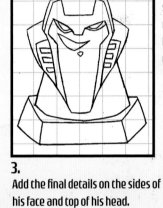

3.
Add the final details on the sides of his face and top of his head.

6.

Finish the drawing by adding further details to Starscream's body and wings. Now just add colour and this Decepticon will be ready to blast off.

The Jet

Keep your eyes on the sky: Starscream is watching. He can transform into a jet and blast through the air at unbelievable speeds.

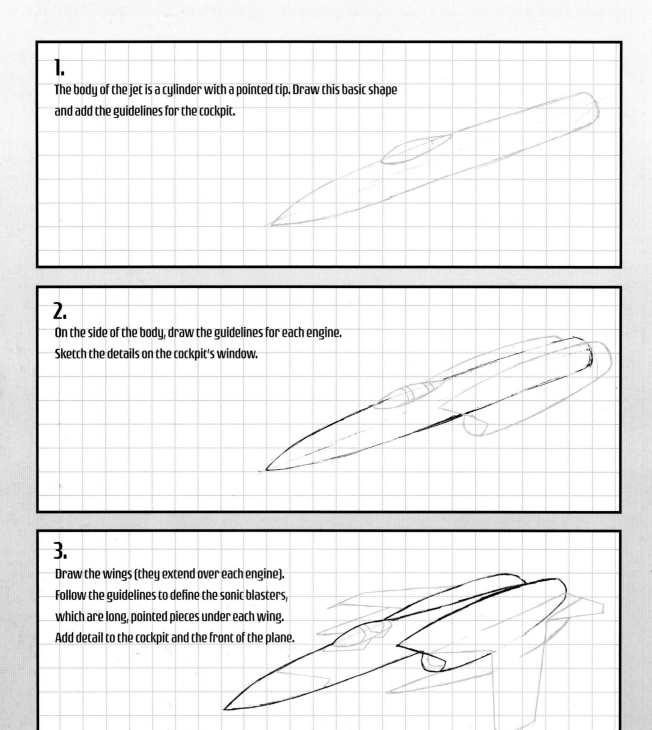

1.
The body of the jet is a cylinder with a pointed tip. Draw this basic shape and add the guidelines for the cockpit.

2.
On the side of the body, draw the guidelines for each engine. Sketch the details on the cockpit's window.

3.
Draw the wings (they extend over each engine). Follow the guidelines to define the sonic blasters, which are long, pointed pieces under each wing. Add detail to the cockpit and the front of the plane.

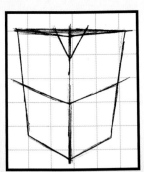

1.
The Decepticon symbol looks like a robot's face. Begin by drawing the basic shape. Don't forget the guidelines for the features!

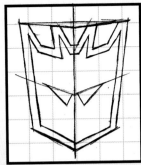

2.
Add two triangles for eyes and a border around the inside of the shape. There should be four points on the top of the face.

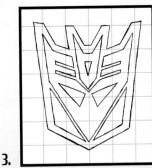

3.
Finish the symbol by adding details. Don't forget to add two triangles at the bottom and four lines above the eyes.

4.
On top of each engine, sketch a fin-like shape. Add the details around the engine and blasters to give your picture depth.

5.
Finally, draw the fine details on the rest of the aircraft. Don't forget the stripe on each wing or the torpedoes hidden above each engine!

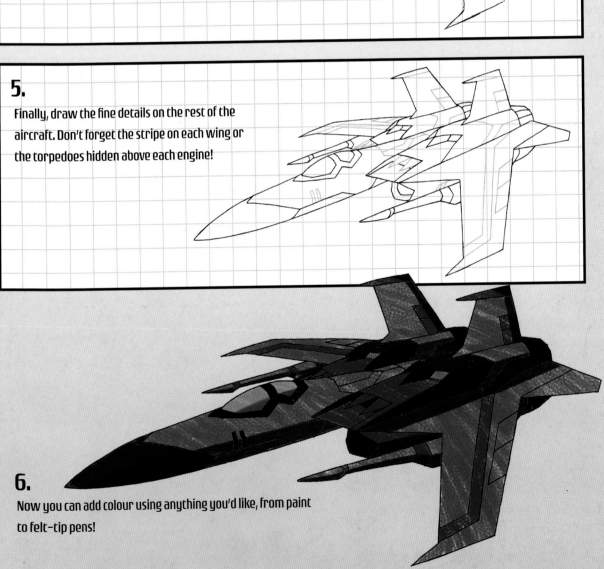

6.
Now you can add colour using anything you'd like, from paint to felt-tip pens!

Ratchet

Short-tempered and grizzled, this Autobot is the team's doctor and Prime's second in command. Ratchet can create magnetic force fields. This helps when patching up the circuitry of Autobots who have been injured in the field. While he's technically not a combat bot, you don't want to get on his bad side. He has a serious attitude problem and can kick chrome with the best of them.

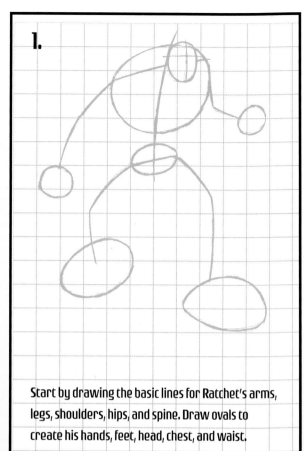

1.

Start by drawing the basic lines for Ratchet's arms, legs, shoulders, hips, and spine. Draw ovals to create his hands, feet, head, chest, and waist.

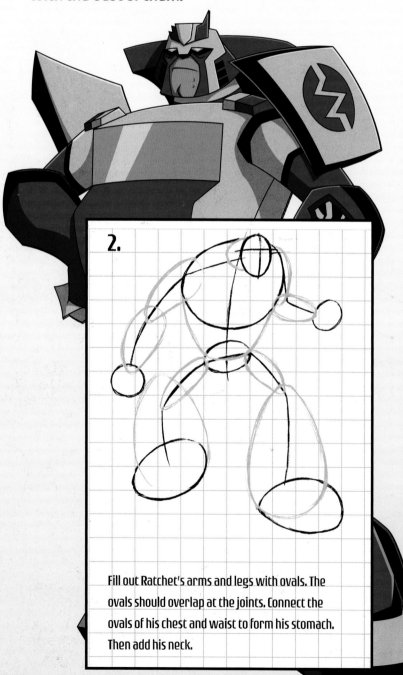

2.

Fill out Ratchet's arms and legs with ovals. The ovals should overlap at the joints. Connect the ovals of his chest and waist to form his stomach. Then add his neck.

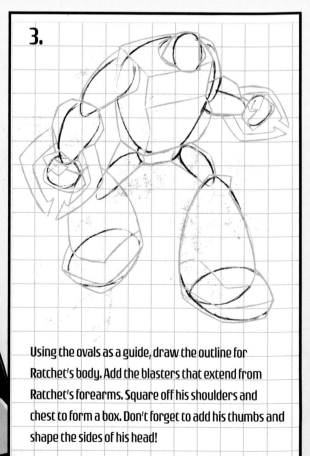

3.

Using the ovals as a guide, draw the outline for Ratchet's body. Add the blasters that extend from Ratchet's forearms. Square off his shoulders and chest to form a box. Don't forget to add his thumbs and shape the sides of his head!

4.

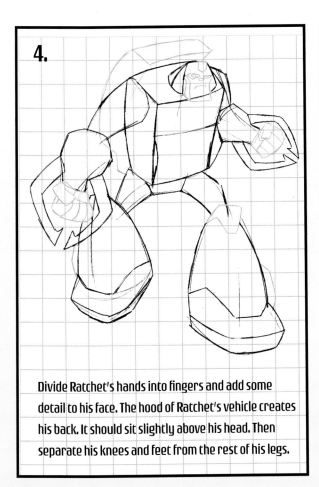

Divide Ratchet's hands into fingers and add some detail to his face. The hood of Ratchet's vehicle creates his back. It should sit slightly above his head. Then separate his knees and feet from the rest of his legs.

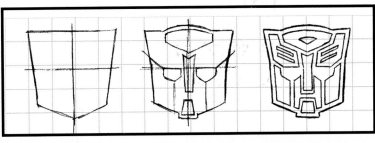

1.

The Autobot symbol looks like a robot's face. Start by drawing this basic shape and the guidelines for the features.

2.

Add the eyes, nose, forehead, and mouth. The top of the symbol curves slightly.

3.

Finish up by adding some final details. Now Autobots . . . roll out!

6.

It's time to give Ratchet his finishing touches. Add the rest of the details as well as the Medic logo on his shoulder. Colour him in using your art supplies.

5.

The sides of his vehicle should sit above his shoulders. Draw the basic shapes for those pieces and add the details on his legs. Don't forget to add the lines on the sides of his face!

The Ambulance

Don't be fooled! Ratchet's secret identity may look like any other ambulance, but no human doctor can harness magnetic energy the way he can.

1.

Begin by drawing the basic shape of the body of the ambulance. Sketch slanted lines to create the bumper, hood, windshield, and roof.

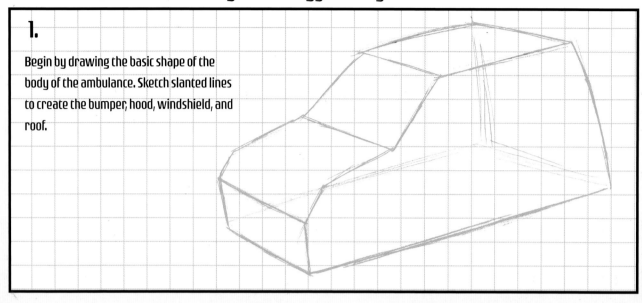

2.

Add guidelines for the windshield and the roof. Sketch two curved rectangles in the side of the body for the wheels.

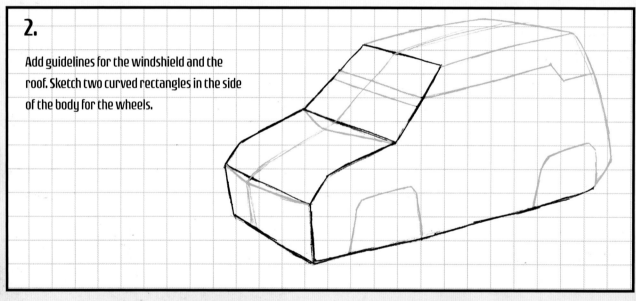

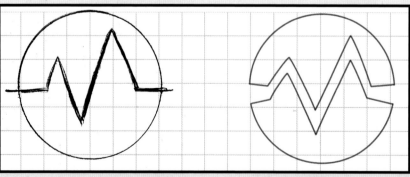

1.
The symbol on the side of Ratchet's truck is just a circle with a zigzag inside it.

2.
Draw another zigzag beside it. Erase all the lines you don't need and darken the rest.

3.

Draw two ovals for each wheel, and add a light above the windshield. Sketch the guidelines on the bumper and the side of the ambulance. Don't forget the circle on the side! This will become the medical symbol.

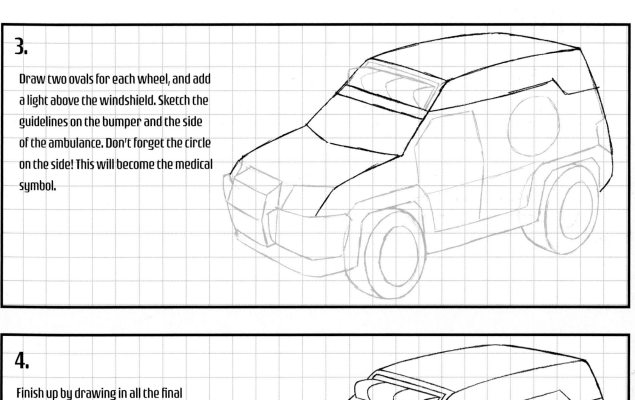

4.

Finish up by drawing in all the final details. The lights on the bumper, the treads on the tyres, and the handles on the side doors will all help make this vehicle look real.

5.

Using the picture of the truck shown here, give your drawing some colour!

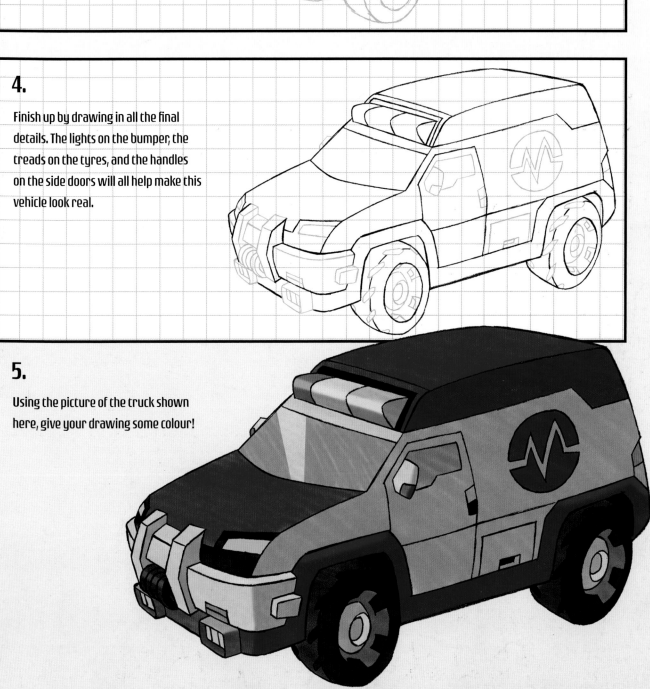

Bulkhead

Bulkhead is the muscle of the Autobot team. His battering-ram arms and wrecking ball make him the perfect demolition bot. demolition On the battlefield he's your greatest weapon, but everywhere else ... well, hide anything breakable.

This gentle giant has a lot of heart. Using these simple steps, draw Bulkhead's expression when he's laughing.

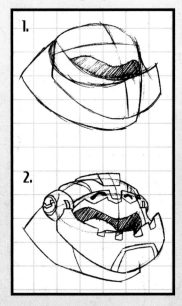

1.

Start by drawing the basic lines that form Bulkhead's arms, legs, shoulders, hips, and spine. Add a rounded triangle for one hand and ovals for his head, chest, and waist. Draw flattened ovals for his feet. Add the guidelines for his face.

2.

Fill out Bulkhead's enormous body by drawing ovals on his arms and legs. Give him a circle for each shoulder. Connect his chest to his waist using curved lines. Then add a curved line below his waist to form his suit.

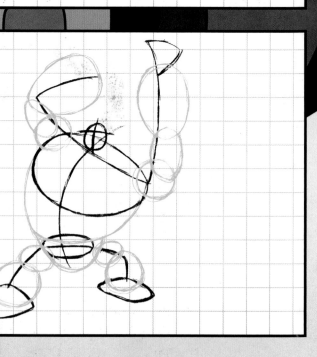

3.

Using the ovals as a guide, outline Bulkhead's body. Draw a line across his waist and lines separating his arms from his chest. Add a circle and a curved line for his wrecking ball. Lastly, define his chin and thumbs.

4.

Draw the details on Bulkhead's body. Add five small circles on the surface of his wrecking ball and add lines to separate his feet from his legs. Bulkhead's most unique feature is his deep, wide jaw. It's almost a half circle, but not quite.

5.

Finish drawing Bulkhead by giving more detail to his body, face, and wrecking ball. Now colour the big guy dark green!

Draw Bulkhead when he's smiling.

1.

2.

Draw Bulkhead when he's serious.

1.

2.

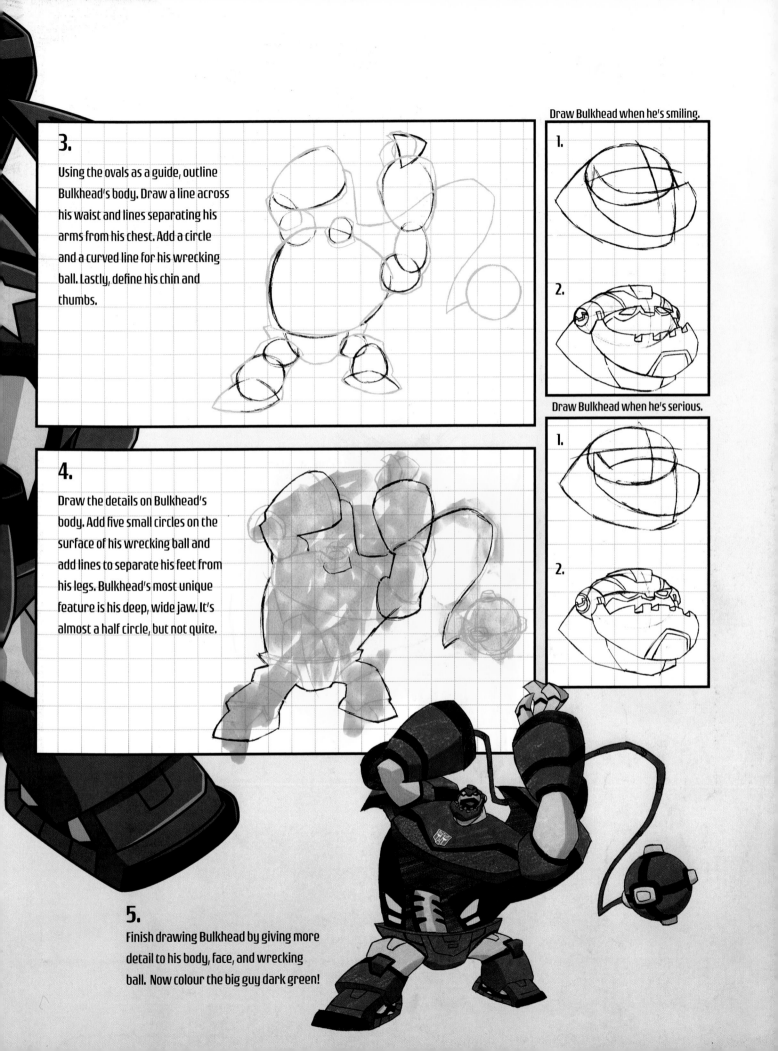

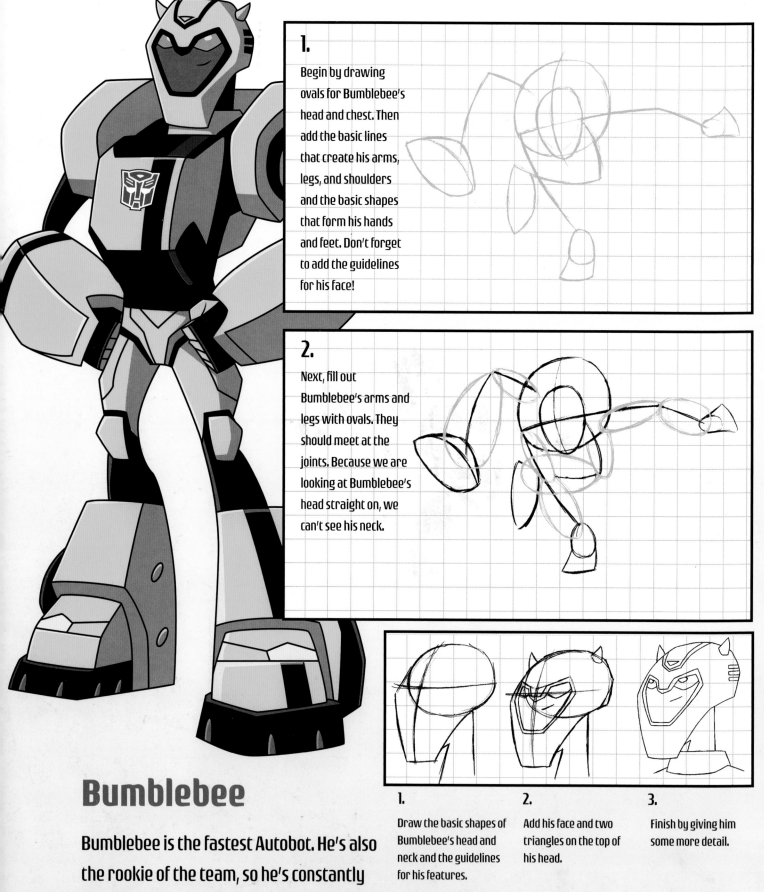

1.

Begin by drawing ovals for Bumblebee's head and chest. Then add the basic lines that create his arms, legs, and shoulders and the basic shapes that form his hands and feet. Don't forget to add the guidelines for his face!

2.

Next, fill out Bumblebee's arms and legs with ovals. They should meet at the joints. Because we are looking at Bumblebee's head straight on, we can't see his neck.

1.
Draw the basic shapes of Bumblebee's head and neck and the guidelines for his features.

2.
Add his face and two triangles on the top of his head.

3.
Finish by giving him some more detail.

Bumblebee

Bumblebee is the fastest Autobot. He's also the rookie of the team, so he's constantly trying to prove himself to the others. Lighthearted and a little immature, Bumblebee loves to make jokes. But when it's time for battle, this Autobot can level the enemy with his powerful energy blasts.

3.

Using the ovals as a guide, draw the outline of Bumblebee's body. Add the basic shapes for Bumblebee's shoulders, and separate his thumbs from his hands. Draw three straight lines to flatten out his chin.

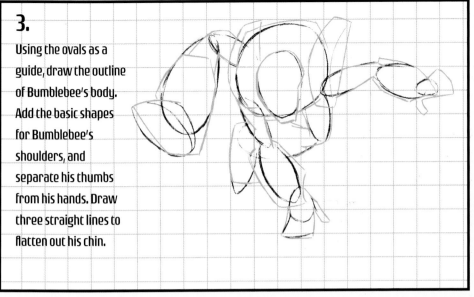

1.

This Autobot has a secret weapon that shoots out from his hand. To draw Bumblebee's stinger, start by sketching these basic shapes.

4.

Bumblebee is a funny bot, so give him a smiling expression. Then, add some more detail on his arms and legs.

2.

Finish by adding the details. Watch out, villains!

5.

Finish your drawing by adding the details on his body and head. Don't forget to add the markings and horns on the top and side of his head. Now colour this Autobot a brilliant yellow!

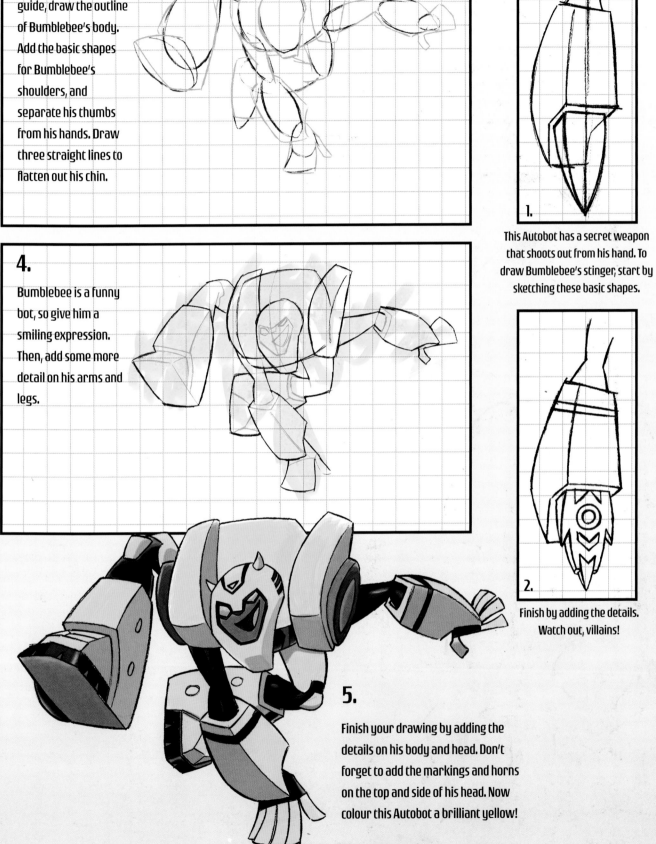

The Racecar

Bumblebee's secret identity is a small, speeding racecar.
Follow the steps below to disguise this Autobot.

1.

Begin by drawing the basic shapes of the car.
Add a guideline for the front corner.

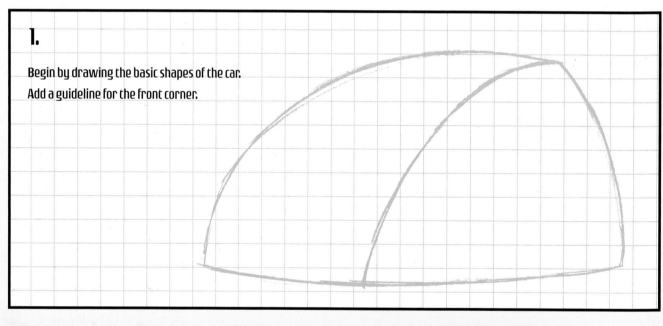

2.

Now draw the curved lines that form
the windshield and side windows. Add
the bumper and two thin ovals for
the wheels. Don't forget to add
Bumblebee's headlights!

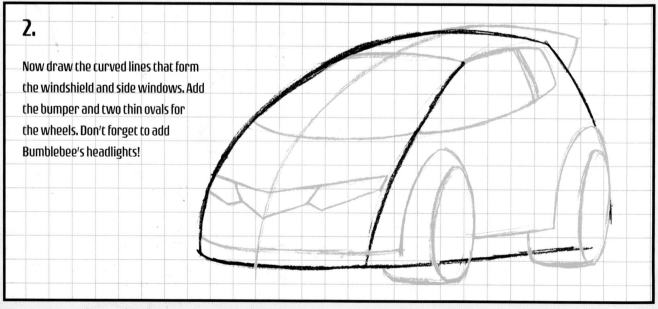

3.

To make this car look real, add rearview mirrors and the details on the wheels. Unlike most of the other vehicles, Bumblebee has smooth tyres. Add the detail on the bumper and use three curved lines to draw the light on top.

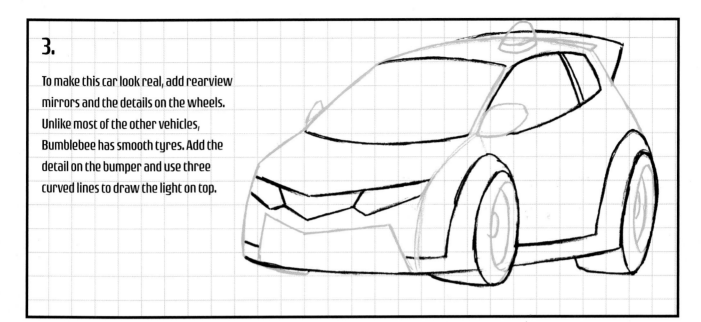

4.

Finish your drawing by adding the stripes on the hood and roof of the car and the highlight on the windshield. Finally, draw the details on the bumper, door, and tyres.

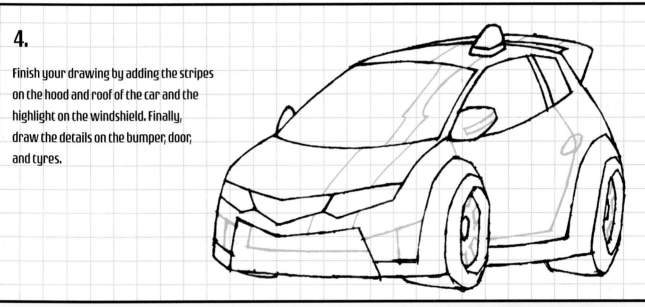

5.

Now give this racecar a sleek paint job!

Transformers Touch Down on Earth

Now that you've learned how to draw all your favourite *Transformers Animated* characters, put your new skills to work by decorating greeting cards, book covers, nametags, and more. Try making your own wrapping paper or comic strips. There's no limit to what you can do when you have the Autobots on your side!

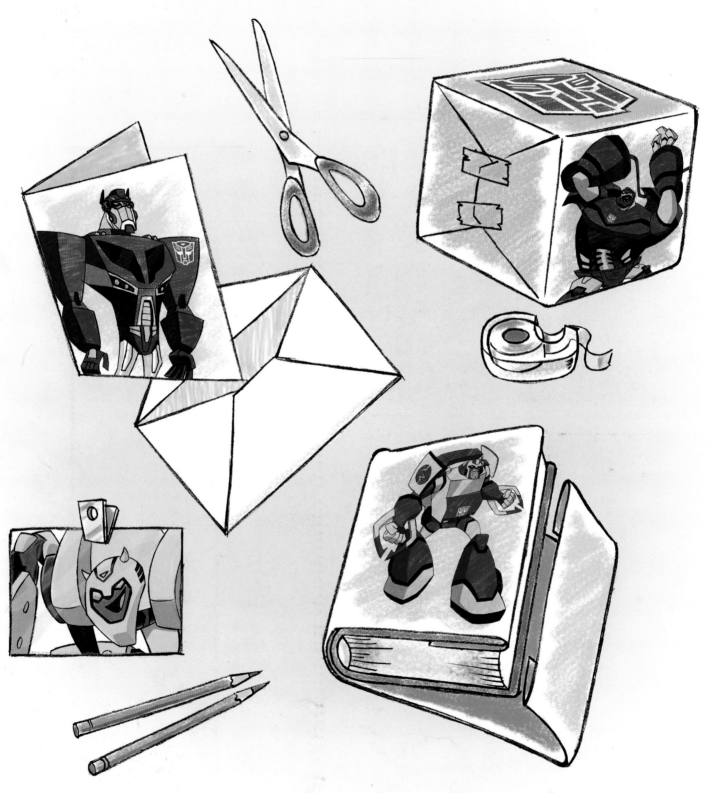